FREIGHT TRAINS OF THE WESTERN REGION IN THE 1980s

Kevin Redwood

AMBERLEY

First published 2020

Amberley Publishing
The Hill, Stroud
Gloucestershire, GL5 4EP

www.amberley-books.com

Copyright © Kevin Redwood, 2020

The right of Kevin Redwood to be identified
as the Author of this work has been asserted in
accordance with the Copyrights, Designs and
Patents Act 1988.

ISBN 978 1 3981 0050 3 (print)
ISBN 978 1 3981 0051 0 (ebook)

British Library Cataloguing in Publication Data.
A catalogue record for this book is available from
the British Library.

Typesetting by Aura Technology and Software
Services, India. Printed in the UK.

Introduction

The photos in this book were taken across the Western Region from 1980 to 1989. The West Country features prominently, as does the Bristol area where I worked for much of my railway career. This book would not have been possible without the help of my friend and BR colleague, Roland Carp. Roland kindly did the driving on a number of occasions so that we could visit some of the more remote locations. He also made his photos available for this book, many of them taken towards the end of the decade. I have credited his photos (RLC).

Freight trains have fascinated me for as long as I can remember. As a child our house in Exeter was near to Exmouth Junction shed and yard, and close enough to hear the shunting, from which I developed a life-long interest in freight trains. My father, Norman Redwood, worked for the Western Region civil engineer's department, and his job often took him to yards and depots across the region. During school holidays I sometimes went with him. From him I learnt about wagons in the civil engineer's fleet, such as dogfish, catfish, mermaids, and sealion hoppers.

After joining BR in 1977 I soon moved to work in the Bristol Area Freight Centre, and from 1980 onwards would use some of my days off to take photos, particularly of freight trains. My railway career was mostly spent based in the West Country, but I often visited South Wales including locations around Newport and Cardiff.

Freight traffic across the Western Region changed greatly during the decade. In 1980 large numbers of vacuum-braked and unfitted wagons were still in traffic, most of them owned by BR. The vacuum-braked wagon-load network was still in operation and served traditional freight terminals and coal depots, which were decreasing in number. Domestic coal, scrap, china clay and cement were among the last commodities to be carried. As new air-braked vehicles entered traffic the vacuum-braked wagon-load network was run down and finally ceased operating in May 1984.

The air-braked Speedlink network had its origins in a combined Freightliner/ air-braked service between Bristol and Glasgow that had started running in 1977. The Speedlink network grew rapidly at the start of the 1980s, as BR introduced new air-braked vehicles, and many freight customers also bought or hired their own fleets of new vehicles. Severn Tunnel Junction became a major Speedlink hub yard with trunk services running to every Region of BR.

On the London Division the major marshalling yards were at Acton and Reading West Junction and, as the freight network contracted the yards, had to adapt to take on new roles. Acton yard was not to become part of the Speedlink network and was heavily rationalised; a reduced number of reception roads were retained to handle aggregates traffic to London and the South East. Reading West Junction yard became the principle yard for engineering trains on the Division.

In the west of England freight traffic varied greatly across the Division. Clay was the most important traffic from the West Country, china clay in Cornwall and Marsh Mills, with ball clay from locations in Devon. The distinctive clayhoods were used for export traffic via Fowey; they were eventually replaced by new CDAs in 1987. For domestic clay traffic to other locations across BR a fleet of clayfits modified with roller bearings had been used. These were replaced in the early 1980s by a variety of privately owned air-braked vehicles. Aggregates traffic from the Mendips and Tytherington initially passed in a variety of BR-owned vehicles, including HTVs and MSVs, but increasingly privately owned vehicles such as PGAs and PTAs were used. In the Bristol and Avonmouth area there were a number of important freight customers handling a wide variety of traffic using different wagon types.

The South Wales Division was by far the busiest division for freight traffic with coal, steel, and petroleum products among the most important. During the 1970s there had been over sixty rail-connected collieries, and there was also a lot of coal traffic between collieries, washeries, and coking plants. However, ongoing closures meant that only six deep mines remained by the end of 1989. British Steel operated a number of important plants and again there was also a lot of inter-works steel traffic for BR. Oil refineries, including those at Milford Haven, provided a lot of petroleum traffic. It was in South Wales that the use of unfitted wagons continued long after they had been phased out elsewhere – coil to Newport Docks, coke to Barry Docks, and coal to Swansea Docks being among the last traffic flows to use unfitted wagons. The changing patterns of freight traffic, combined with colliery closures, meant that there were yard and branch closures taking place throughout the decade. The major yards at Severn Tunnel Junction closed completely in October 1987, something that would have been unthinkable at the start of the decade. Other yards such as Margam and Llandeilo Junction would also see major rationalisation.

The locomotive fleet would also see great change with a number of classes becoming extinct during the decade. For shunting duties, the WR had a small number of Class 03s in Bristol and at Landore (for use in West Wales), though in both cases they were replaced by Class 08s. The Class 08 locos were widely used across the region for shunting and marshalling and in places for local freight trip work. The WR allocation of Class 31s tended to be used on local freight trips, and frequently on civil engineers' trains, including midweek ballast drops. Class 37 locos became synonymous with freight trains in South Wales, particularly in the valleys, and a smaller number of the class worked clay traffic in the South West. The Class 47 fleet were found across the region working all types of traffic, whereas the Class 50s were less often seen on freight work. The Western Region allocation of Class 56s tended to work iron ore, and petroleum traffic in South Wales. Aggregates traffic was also worked by the Class 56s, and from 1986 they were joined by the privately owned Class 59s on traffic from the Mendips. Foreign visitors of Classes 20, 33, 40, 45, and 58 all worked freight services onto the Western Region.

Choosing the photos and carrying out the research for this book has brought back many happy memories. Thanks again to Roland Carp for his help and the use of his photos. All the other photos were taken by me, with one by my late brother Steve. Once again, I must thank my partner, Antoinette, for her support as I worked on this book, and my mother, Ruth Redwood, for putting up with me talking about trains for sixty years.

Class 31s were often used on engineers' train. Here No. 31321 approaches Acton Main Line with a short trip from Westbourne Park on 11 April 1983. The three grampus wagons are well loaded with what appears to be general rubbish. In problem areas special trains were occasionally run to clear fly-tipped rubbish from the lineside.

The Great Western main line saw a lot of inter-regional freight traffic. At Acton Main Line is Thornaby-allocated No. 47361 with a westbound Freightliner service on 11 April 1983. The train is 4O79, the 09.55 from Ripple Lane to Southampton Maritime, which had been routed over the North London Line.

Acton Yard was the originating point for inter-regional services to the London Midland, Eastern, and Southern Regions. On 11 April 1983 Hither Green-allocated No. 33060 is departing the yard for the Southern Region with a vacuum-braked service, which includes 16t mineral wagons and some engineer's vehicles. The two-character headcode 'KI' should indicate a service from the Western Region to Bricklayers Arms if correctly displayed.

Bath Road-allocated No. 47059 stands in Acton Yard with a loaded train of MSVs (in TOPS pool 7609) on 11 April 1983. Large numbers of these wagons were employed to convey aggregates from the Mendip quarries to terminals in London and the South East. By the end of the decade much of Acton Yard had been closed, those sidings which remained were those nearest the main line and were principally used for aggregates traffic.

Acton Yard had not been selected as a Speedlink Trunk Yard. Consequently, as the traditional vacuum-braked wagon-load network contracted, so Acton Yard declined in importance. On 2 November 1983 there is not much traffic in evidence, and a number of sidings have already been taken out of use. After rationalisation only half a dozen sidings survived, these were next to the main line, those on the right of this view from the west end.

Bath Road depot first received an allocation of Class 56 locos in 1982, and by 1986 there were thirteen members of the class in use principally on aggregates traffic. On 5 March 1986 No. 56055 heads west through Reading with 6V84 the 09.xx from Allington to Stoke Gifford with thirty-six empty PGAs for ARC Tytherington Quarry. (RLC)

Although there were no Class 20s allocated to the Western Region, members of the class were visitors to the region on freight services. On 6 February 1986 on a bitterly cold day, with a temperature of minus three degrees Celsius, Toton-allocated Nos 20188 and 20059 are seen light engine(s) at Reading. (RLC)

Departing from Didcot on the Up relief line on 10 July 1981 is No. 47243 with a vacuum-braked service, nearest the camera are four 21t hoppers (TOPS code HTV). The train is probably a Bescot to Eastleigh service, which had just called at Didcot for traincrew relief.

In the early 1980s Cardiff Canton had an allocation of around sixty Class 47s, the majority of which had no train heating, and were largely employed on freight work. One of the allocation No. 47075 heads east through Didcot with a tank train on 17 November 1982.

The majority of stone trains from the Mendip quarries to London and the South East ran up the Berks & Hants route via Newbury. At times some services ran via Melksham, as in this instance on 8 July 1985. A set of loaded tipplers (TOPS code PTA) from ARC Whatley quarry runs into Didcot behind No. 47246, which was a Bath Road-allocated loco.

A number of freight services were booked to take traincrew relief at Didcot. Here on 17 November 1982 is 4S59, a Southampton Maritime to Coatbridge Freightliner service seen calling at Didcot behind loco No. 47100.

The Cardiff Canton-allocated Class 56 loco diagrams included working petroleum trains from the Milford Haven refineries. Passing Didcot behind No. 56041 is 6B27, a train of discharged tanks from the Murco depot at Theale returning to Robeston on 8 July 1985.

The yards at Reading West Junction were the focal point for civil engineer's trains on the London Division. Old Oak Common-allocated No. 31296 is working a midweek ballast drop from Reading on 17 November 1982. It is seen propelling the train of seven loaded sealions and seacows around the West Curve at Didcot. The train is signalled onto the Up main line where it will carry out the ballast drop on the return run to Reading.

Class 58 locos were introduced in 1983. All fifty members of the class were allocated to Toton depot and they were commonly found working MGR trains to Didcot Power Station. Rounding the West Curve at Didcot is No. 58002 with a loaded train on 8 July 1985. The maximum permitted load for Didcot varied depending on the route but could be up to forty-five wagons.

Wearing the recently introduced Railfreight grey livery is Cricklewood-allocated No. 31128. It is running into Didcot yard on 8 July 1985 with a train of ZHVs. The wagons are 16t mineral wagons which had been transferred to the civil engineer's fleet for loading spoil and spent ballast. In this use they were regularly overloaded, so rectangular holes were cut in the sides to prevent overloading.

Approaching Oxford, an unidentified Class 56 loco heads northwards with an empty MGR train from Didcot Power Station on 10 July 1981. The introduction of this class of loco enabled heavier trains to be run compared to the Class 47s that had previously been used. For example, from Toton to Didcot a Class 56 could haul forty-five HAAs, compared to a maximum load of thirty-six for a Class 47.

Although Class 58 locos were principally used on merry-go-round coal trains, they did find work on other traffic. Earlier on 8 July 1985 No. 58025 had worked south through Oxford with a Freightliner service. It is seen heading back north with empty cartic wagons from Hinksey Yard.

The first Class 58 loco was delivered from Doncaster Works in December 1982, with the final loco of the fifty members of the class entering service in 1987. The first loco to enter service, No. 58001, is seen heading north at Oxford on 8 July 1985 with an empty MGR train from Didcot Power Station.

The 1987 WR Freight Train Loads Book listed the following collieries and yards that sent trains to Didcot Power Station: Baddesley, Bagworth, Barrow Hill, Bescot, Birch Coppice, Coalfield Farm, Coventry Colliery, Daw Mill, Desford, Kingsbury, Mantle Lane, Marhkam, Three Spires, Toton, and Washwood Heath. That is in addition to loading points in South Wales. On 8 July 1985 No. 58001 powers southwards through Oxford with a loaded train for Didcot Power Station.

At the start of the 1980s Class 56 locos were the preferred power for MGR trains to Didcot, being more powerful than the Class 47s they replaced. The increase in train length varied from between three and fifteen additional wagons, depending on the route. Passing Oxford on 6 February 1986 is No. 56071 working 6M75 11.05 Didcot PS to Coalfields Farm. (RLC)

As well as the significant trainload freight passing through Oxford there was still some local wagon load traffic, notably to the freight depot at Morris Cowley. On 13 April 1983 one of the Reading-allocated Class 08s, No. 08946, heads north through Oxford with a pair of VTG ferry wagons. In the distance No. 47462 is working the 06.25 Poole to Liverpool Lime Street service.

Until the more powerful Class 56 locos were introduced in 1976 MGR trains to Didcot Power Station were worked by Class 47s. However, Class 47s continued to work some services to Didcot into the 1980s, even though they could only handle a reduced load. On 13 April 1983 one of the large Bescot allocation of 47/3s, No. 47366, heads south through Oxford with a loaded train.

The Ministry of Defence central ordnance depot at Bicester has provided regular traffic for BR. Often a lot of traffic was dispatched at the start of the week and Monday 8 July 1985 was no exception. Passing Oxford is 6A50, the return trip from Bicester behind No. 47217. Behind the loco are six VDAs then two VEAs, a type of short-wheelbase wagon modified specifically for MOD use, as many depots had sidings with tight curves.

A scene at Oxford that would soon become history as a vacuum-braked freight service arrives behind Toton-allocated No. 25308 on 10 July 1981. The train is 8V33, the 11.45 MWFO Banbury to Oxford service. The leading wagons are loaded with house coal for either Oxford Rewley Road or Abingdon, while the long rake of empty coal wagons had been attached at Betchington Cement Works. The loco would later work back to Banbury with 7M36 the 15.47 departure from Oxford South Yard.

The small loco depot at Swindon had an allocation of Class 08 shunting locos to shunt in Swindon Works, and at the various yards and terminals at Swindon. One of the allocation, No. 08795, is seen in Swindon station on 4 September 1984. It is making a shunt move from Cocklebury Yard across the main lines to Swindon Transfer Sidings on the south side of the main line.

Speedlink route 1 connected South Wales with Dover and Essex. Here 6E91, the 14.10 Severn Tunnel Junction to Ripple Lane Speedlink service, passes Swindon behind Immingham-allocated No. 47314 on 4 September 1984. Behind the loco is a VCA and then three cartic sets which are returning empty to the Fords plant at Dagenham Dock.

The first Class 37 locos allocated to Bath Road depot arrived in 1978 and they were put to work on stone traffic. Two pairs were required to work the two weekday stone trains from ARC Tytherington to Wolverton. On 4 September 1984 Nos 37204 and 37158 are passing Swindon with 6V11, the 09.10 Wolverton to Stoke Gifford return working conveying empty PGAs.

On 25 March 1980 Gateshead-allocated No. 46035 arrives at Worcester Shrub Hill with 8V61 a vacuum-braked freight service from Bescot to Gloucester New Yard, which conveys a mixed load. At the start of 1980 Laira depot also had an allocation of twenty-five members of the class, but they were all withdrawn or transferred to Gateshead before the end of the year.

At the start of the 1980s the Western Region civil engineer's wagon fleet still contained large numbers of unfitted wagons. Consequently, a number of brake vans were still required for use on weekend engineering trains, including some older pre-nationalisation types. Three engineer's brake vans, including a former GWR van, stand in the snow at Worcester Shrub Hill. Photo by my late brother Steve Redwood, probably taken during the winter of 1981/82. (SJR)

By 1982 although there was not much revenue-earning freight traffic to or from Worcester there was also sufficient civil engineer's traffic to justify the provision of a Class 08 yard pilot. On 12 February 1982, one of four Class 08 locos allocated to Gloucester No. 08778 is at work at Worcester Shrub Hill. It is shunting a rake of engineer's grampus wagons. In the next siding are some brand new seacow ballast hoppers.

Heading through Gloucester on 10 July 1985 is No. 37172 with 7B12 16.55 Gloucester New Yard to Severn Tunnel Junction Speedlink service. In October 1987 a major change to the Speedlink network on the Western Region took place when the yards at Severn Tunnel Junction closed, and Gloucester New Yard was one of several locations that received extra work as a result.

On 4 September 1984 Immingham-allocated No. 47312 heads north through Gloucester with an empty Freightliner working. A variety of locos can be seen on Horton Road depot, including Nos 45141, 37135, 37282 and 37036. The depot here often hosted visiting locos from other regions.

Gloucester saw a lot of freight traffic passing between the Midlands and South Wales. Bescot-allocated No. 47060 passes through with 6Z20, a special working from Tinsley to Cardiff Tidal on 10 July 1985. The BDA wagons are loaded with billets of steel for Allied Steel & Wire at Cardiff.

Class 20s were regularly seen working between the Midlands and South Wales, as seen here on 10 July 1985. Tinsley-allocated pair Nos 20115 and 20022 are working 6Z45, a special from Wednesbury Steel Terminal to Cardiff Tidal conveying empty SPA wagons. The wagons are all returning to Allied Steel & Wire at Cardiff for reloading with steel products.

In the early evening of 10 July 1985 No. 37189 climbs into Gloucester with a very mixed freight service from Severn Tunnel Junction. Behind the loco are several items of civil engineer's on-track equipment with associated messing and tool vans, with various other traffic marshalled behind.

The Dow-Mac works at Quedgeley, south of Gloucester, produced concrete products including concrete sleepers for BR. The sleepers had previously been dispatched to BR pre-assembly depots (PADs) loaded in tube wagons. By the mid-1980s the loading method was to use bogie wagons with timber battens and nylon straps to secure the load. Dow-Mac staff can be seen adjusting the straps on two sturgeon wagons on 10 July 1985.

In 1973 the former Midland Railway branch to Thornbury had been partially reopened to serve the ARC quarry at Tytherington. Stone traffic was considerable and five or six trips a day ran to and from Stoke Gifford Yard. On 18 September 1989 No. 56032 *Sir De Morgannwg/County of South Glamorgan* rejoins the main line at Yate with loaded PGAs forming the 16.45 trip from Tytherington to Stoke Gifford. (RLC)

Approaching Stoke Gifford Down loop on 30 May 1985 is No. 56065, working 6B83 from Tytherington, which unusually is formed of only three loaded bogie tippler wagons (PTAs). A train of loaded PGAs from Tytherington is standing on the adjacent Down reception line. Class 56 locos first appeared on Tytherington stone trains during 1982 when Bath Road depot first received an allocation of ten members of the class. (RLC)

Although most of the former Up yard at Stoke Gifford had been turned into a car park the Up loop and Up reception remained in use. Services on the Tytherington branch were timed to avoid using the crossing over the Iron Acton by-pass during the rush hours. So 6B82, worked by No. 45101, will depart at 08.55 for Tytherington, the empty MSVs will then be loaded for either Appleford or Oxford Banbury Road. The date is 10 July 1985.

A general view of Stoke Gifford yard on 7 September 1983. On the Up loop is No. 47072 with a vacuum-braked freight from Severn Tunnel Junction to Acton Yard. In Stoke Gifford Down side yard are two rakes of MSVs, former 26t iron ore tipplers by now in use on stone traffic from Tytherington. The two missing sidings were subsequently reinstated in the gap when additional Speedlink traffic was handled at Stoke Gifford.

Project Mercury was a scheme in the early 1980s to lay fibre optic cabling alongside part of the British Rail network. In Bristol the trains were usually formed of a rake of modified pipe wagons with a brake van at each end working out of Kingsland Road yard. Class 31 locos were normally allocated to the duty, which ran with a headcode of 7Z01, and on 10 July 1985 No. 31168 is seen leaving Stoke Gifford Down loop on a return working to Kingsland Road.

With the closure of the vacuum-braked network in 1984 all remaining domestic coal traffic was transferred to Speedlink services and coal from South Wales arrived at Stoke Gifford on 6B18 from Severn Tunnel Junction. On 10 July 1985 No. 47315 arrives at Stoke Gifford. After shunting it will then work local trip No. T77 to Ashton Junction with coal for Wapping Wharf CCD.

One of the first Class 31 locos to be allocated to the Western Region was No. 5535 which was later renumbered as No. 31117. As a long-term resident of Old Oak Common depot, it became a pet loco, and was always well looked after. On 10 July 1985 it arrives at Stoke Gifford with an engineer's ballast drop, with the permanent way gang riding on the seacow ballast wagons.

Approaching Hallen Marsh on 11 February 1980 is No. 37233 with a train largely composed of grampus wagons. The train is heading for St Andrews Road where the civil engineers had established a temporary tip siding. The spoil and spent ballast unloaded at St Andrews Road tip was used to raise the level of the land, and this later became the site of the reception sidings for the Bristol Bulk Handling Terminal.

Passing Hallen Marsh signal box is No. 45013 with 7V66 Tees Yard to ICI Severnside; the wagons are loaded with potash from Boulby. This train started running as a company train but later became part of the Speedlink network and then conveyed other traffic en route. In the column road on the left is No. 08949, which had been specially provided at Hallen Marsh that day, 5 October 1983, in connection with a trial load of fertiliser from Ince and Elton to the PBA Chittening Estate.

A regular freight traffic was confectionary from Rowntrees at Fosse Islands, in York, to various warehouses across the country including Avonmouth Town. The 'chocolate engine' (as trip No. 78 was known) passes Hallen Marsh signal box on the return trip after shunting at Avonmouth, with No. 47286 propelling on 5 October 1983. This propelling movement required a brake van to lead the move, and was not permitted during darkness, fog, or falling snow.

One of Commonwealth Smelting Company's 4wDH Sentinel shunting locos is seen on 26 Jan 1982. It is crossing the busy Smoke Lane crossing with a train of coke in HTVs. The Smelting Works at Hallen Marsh received coke from South Wales each weekday, latterly supplied from the BSC Margam Abbey Works.

The Commonwealth Smelting Company works were connected to the BR network at Hallen Marsh by the inwards and outwards lines. On 5 February 1982 No. 37255 draws slowly out to Hallen Marsh with 7C42 for Severn Tunnel Junction. Behind the loco are three VDAs loaded with zinc ingots for Bloxwich. The bulk of the train is made up of empty hoppers which had arrived loaded with coke.

In 1964 BR made a determined bid to capture a share of the clay traffic to the Potteries, and the first of the daily 'Clayliner' trains started running from St Blazey to the Potteries in 1965. The return working from Stoke-on-Trent, the 6V53 to St Blazey, became a familiar and much photographed train. Here on 30 September 1981 6V53 passes through Stapleton Road behind No. 47318. From 1982 the four-wheel wooden-bodied clayfits were replaced by a fleet of thirty-five new PBA Polybulks, known as clay tigers.

A pair of Class 37s pass one another beneath the former Midland Railway bridge at Lawrence Hill on 22 April 1981. A southbound service from Severn Tunnel Junction passes on the main line behind No. 37275. Meanwhile, creeping out of Lawrence Hill yard is No. 37277 with 7C62, the 16.35 service to Severn Tunnel Junction.

On 6 April 1980 No. 37071 has arrived at Lawrence Hill to work the 7C62 departure for Severn Tunnel Junction as yard pilot No. 03382 shunts to form up the train. The yard was busy with cement in bulk and in bags which were unloaded in the goods shed. A Class 03 loco was diagrammed on this duty as it was also required to shunt the Avonside branch, over which only Class 03 locos were permitted at the time.

By 1981 Bath Road no longer had an allocation of Class 03 locos as Class 08s were now permitted to shunt on Avonside Wharf. On 22 April 1981 No. 08338 is the Lawrence Hill yard pilot. It is seen shunting to form up 7C62 for Severn Tunnel Junction. The vans are in a pool for conveying bagged cement between Aberthaw Cement works and Lawrence Hill and are covered in cement dust.

On 28 September 1983 Lawrence Hill yard pilot No. 08949 is seen at Barton Road Crossing on the Avonside Branch. It is propelling a rake of TTAs loaded with molasses from King's Lynn for the Distillers Company plant on Avonside Wharf. The shunters are riding on another brake van at the head of the train controlling the propelling move. In later years when rail traffic become infrequent it was not unusual to find parked cars blocking the crossing.

The Avonside Branch was part of the remains of the former Midland Railway network in Bristol, it still served the Distillers Company plant and the Blue Circle Cement depot on Avonside Wharf. On 28 September 1983 the shunters control the traffic on Avon Street Crossing as Lawrence Hill pilot No. 08949 propels molasses tanks onto the Wharf.

Although there were no Speedlink trunk services through Bristol there were several important Speedlink feeder services, including 6O42 08.30 Severn Tunnel Junction to Eastleigh. This service often saw a Class 45 loco work to Eastleigh as on 28 September 1983 when 6O42 passes through Lawrence Hill behind Toton-allocated No. 45051.

A view of Kingsland Road Yard in Bristol looking towards Temple Meads station on 20 September 1983. All of the marshalling yards in Bristol had closed, or been adapted, for other use, so Kingsland Road undertook local sorting of traffic as well as being a full loads freight depot. Guinness is being unloaded from vans on the left. The sidings in the middle are used for marshalling, and on the right, across the main lines, is part of Barton Hill wagon repair depot.

On 20 September 1983 Kingsland Road pilot No. 08950 is sorting Speedlink traffic which has recently arrived. The VCAs are loaded with Enparts loco stores, and the BDA contains a switch and crossing for the civil engineers. The brake van was semi-permanently attached to the yard pilot at Kingsland Road. It was regular practice at several locations in Bristol for a pilot loco to work with a brake van attached.

The Bristol Enparts tripper was diagrammed to be worked by a Bath Road Class 08 loco. It would work stores, vans and fuel tanks between Bath Road, Marsh Junction, the HST depot, Kingsland Road and Malago Vale (as required). On 20 September No. 08819 is on Enparts duty and is seen at Kingsland Road with three Enparts VCAs of loco stores, from Swindon and Crewe works, and a TTA of lubricating oil for Bath Road.

A curiosity of the Bristol freight scene was the pair of Malago 'muck trucks'. These were two lowmac wagons that had been modified to convey waste skips. These were used to move bags of carriage cleaning waste from Malago Vale carriage sidings (where there was no road access), to Kingsland Road. On 20 September 1983 No. 45057, on local freight trip duty, has arrived at Kingsland Road with one of the lowmacs to be emptied.

In the Speedlink era BR worked with a number of private firms to handle cartage and cranage at various yards. Premier Transport worked at Kingsland Road in Bristol and also at Exeter. On 20 September 1983 VGAs of Guinness from Park Royal are being unloaded at Kingsland Road.

A long-lived pair of trains ran to convey steel traffic between South Wales and Hamworthy, conveying finished and semi-finished steel both for import and export. On 16 June 1986 No. 47236 approaches Bath Spa with 6V99 14.52 Hamworthy to Severn Tunnel Junction. The train comprises fourteen empty vacuum-braked shockhood wagons (TOPS coded OUV).

Passing through Bradford on Avon on 23 August 1983 is No. 37282 with 6V26, the 07.03 Southampton to East Usk. The yard at East Usk was the collecting point for coal empties from across the south and west. From there empties were sent on to collieries and loading points in South Wales as required.

Once the Speedlink network built up there were two daily trains each way between Severn Tunnel Junction and Eastleigh, and they carried a wide variety of traffic. On 16 June 1986 No. 47156 accelerates towards Hawkeridge Junction after the Westbury Yard stop with 6V79 for Severn Tunnel Junction. Behind the loco the VEA and ODAs have probably conveyed MOD traffic; there are TTAs which are loaded with calcium carbonate from Quidhampton, and four discharged bitumen tanks.

The Blue Circle Cement plant at Westbury was located near Heywood Road Junction and provided a lot of traffic for BR. As well as receiving coal the plant sent bulk cement to Southampton, Poole, Hamworthy, Theale, Lawrence Hill, Exeter Central, and Barnstaple. Westbury Yard pilot No. 08951 brings twenty-five loaded presflos into Westbury on 3 January 1981. Rakes of PGAs belonging to ARC are stabled on either side, and on the right preparation work for the construction of Westbury Panel has commenced.

Westbury Panel has already been open for just over two years as No. 47242 passes with a train of empty bogie tipplers for ARC Whatley Quarry on 16 June 1986. These PTA wagons were originally built for imported iron ore to Consett steelworks but rendered surplus by closure of the works in 1981. The wagons were very suitable for aggregates traffic; ARC took fifty of the wagons, and Foster Yeoman hired the remaining seventy-four. They worked in block trains from the Mendips to locations across the South East.

The discharged Murco tanks from Theale to Robeston depart from Westbury behind No. 56032 *Sir De Morgannwg/County of South Glamorgan* on 21 June 1984. In the background is the White House building, which housed the Railway Training School, and the Area Manager Westbury.

The second of the daily Speedlink services from Eastleigh to Severn Tunnel Junction was 6V83 seen here departing from Westbury behind No. 47312 on 21 June 1984. The PCAs behind the loco are flyash empties returning from the Westbury Blue Circle Cement works to Longannet Power Station.

Large numbers of 26t tippler wagons (TOPS code MSV) were used in aggregates traffic from the Mendips, with Class 47s as the principle motive power. On 21 June 1984 No. 47098 arrives at Westbury with the 15.45 trip from ARC Whatley Quarry, with loaded wagons for Fareham. The MSVs were robust wagons that gave many years sterling service, and many were later used by the civil engineers for both ballast and spoil.

Southern Region Class 33s worked some of the services from the Mendips. Here on 21 June 1984 Nos 33009 and 33107 accelerate away from a signal check at Clink Road Junction east of Frome. The train of PGAs is returning empty from Allington to ARC Whatley.

From 1982 Bath Road-allocated Class 56 locos had started working many of the services from the Mendip Quarries. By 1986 there were thirteen members of the class allocated to Bath Road and one of them, No. 56055, is seen at Clink Road Junction with a local trip working from Westbury to Whatley Quarry on 7 July 1986. (RLC)

Foster Yeoman had been unhappy with the reliability of the Class 56 locos and in a major change of policy ordered US-built Class 59 locos from EMD. Four members of the class arrived in January 1986 with a fifth being added later. On 7 July 1986 No. 59003 approaches Clink Road Junction with 6A20, the 17.05 Merehead to Brentford which is formed of loaded PGAs. (RLC)

Meldon Quarry forwarded two trains of ballast to the Southern Region each weekday, and these normally ran up the WR main line to Westbury. Hither Green-allocated 33/2 No. 33201 passes Clink Road Junction on 7 July 1986 with 6O70 from Meldon, which is formed of sealion and seacow hoppers. The Class 33/2 locos were not commonly seen on the Western Region. (RLC)

The Bristol Temple Meads west end pilot No. 08900 draws two air-braked vans out of Temple Meads goods shed on 10 May 1980. The vans are loaded one each for the NCL at Glasgow and Edinburgh, and they will be taken to Kingsland Road. Later they will go to West depot to attach to 4S38, the 18.20 West depot to Glasgow, a joint Freightliner/ABS service that was a forerunner of the Speedlink network.

For a few months in 1983 extensive use was made of Bristol Temple Meads for loading and unloading of cars and small vans that were imported and exported through Portbury Dock. Initial loadings were made from the motorail dock behind platform 2, and on 5 July 1983 Temple Meads west end pilot No. 08951 shunts loaded cartics out onto the Up through line.

The Freightliner terminal at Bristol West depot was not a large one, normally handling two or three five-sets each day. By 1983 it was served by a daily connecting service from Cardiff Pengam. Passing through Temple Meads on 5 August 1983 is 4B48, the 05.20 Pengam to West depot, behind Canton-allocated No. 47257.

Crewe Diesel-allocated No. 47074 passes Bristol Temple Meads heading west on the Down through line with a train of TTAs on 4 March 1980. In the background is Bristol Loco Yard signal box which had closed as a signal box in March 1970. However, the building remained in use and staff there helped control movements on and off Bath Road depot.

Special movements were sometimes arranged as on 17 May 1982 when a repaired dogfish ballast hopper was moved from Weston-super-Mare to Bristol East depot. Wagon No. DB993311 had been loaded at Meldon Quarry but had developed a hot axle box. After temporary repair at Weston it is being hauled through Bristol Temple Meads by trip loco No. 47377, the axle box has again run hot.

Passing Bristol West Junction on 27 April 1983 is 6Z31, the 10.45 Tiverton Junction to Washwood Heath, with discharged tanks for Bromford Bridge. The oil terminal at Tiverton Junction was to close just three days later on 30 April 1983, while No. 46037 would survive until June 1984, by which date only nine members of the class remained in traffic.

Although Royal Portbury Dock had opened in 1977 it was not rail connected until 2002. For a few months in 1983 BR handled import and export car traffic, which had to be brought by road to Bristol. The NCL depot at Pylle Hill was used for some of the loading, and in August 1983 autic and cartic sets can be seen in the loading dock. The sidings at Pylle Hill were normally only used to load *Observer* colour supplements, and for stabling of parcel vans.

Since August 1977 the Ashton Meadows to Wapping Wharf section of the former Bristol Harbour Railway had been operated under agreement by Western Fuel. Each weekday a service brought hoppers of coal from Severn Tunnel Junction to Ashton Meadows, thirty or more could arrive daily in winter. Western Fuel operated a Hudswell Clark shunter, formerly Port of Bristol Authority No. 30, seen here on 11 February 1980. It has just departed Ashton Meadows, heading for Wapping Wharf.

Passing Chelvey near Nailsea and Backwell on 6 November 1986 is Bescot-allocated No. 47060 with 7M53, the 15.00 TTHO Bridgwater to Sellafield, with two loaded nuclear flasks from Hinkley Point. The train will then call at Gloucester New Yard to attach more flasks which had been loaded at Berkeley.

Trainloads of export china clay from Cornwall to Switzerland ran for many years – two trains each of eleven Polybulk hoppers – which returned combined as one train of twenty-two empties. On 26 August 1989 6V24, the 01.50 Dover to Burngullow empty train, passes through Yatton behind No. 47105. (RLC)

Loaded nuclear flasks from Hinkley Point Power Station to Sellafield were loaded to rail at Bridgwater. Since 1981 a special dedicated service had been run between Bridgwater and Sellafield. On 28 September 1989 No. 31200, in Trainload Coal livery, passes the closed box at Hewish Crossing with 7M53, the 16.49 TThO Bridgwater to Sellafield. (RLC)

Passing the site of Bleadon and Uphill station on 27 July 1989 is 6Z14, the 13.15 Heathfield to Waterston discharged tank train. Trainload Freight had been created in 1988, and loco Nos 37280 and 37294 are in Trainload Petroleum livery. The station here had closed in 1964, and for a few years was then home to the small Yieldingtree Railway Museum, which had since closed. (RLC)

During the 1980s as the number of unfitted wagons declined the BR network gradually became a fully fitted railway. To cater for remaining unfitted wagon movements, a small network of Class 9 freight services was run. One of the services was 9B04, the 06.30 WFO Gloucester New Yard to Tavistock Junction, seen on 7 March 1986 at Huntspill behind No. 47258. From Taunton the train was required to run as Class 8 as the West Country had already become a fully fitted railway by that date. (RLC)

The second man looks from the cab of No. 31117 at Huntspill on 7 March 1986. The train is a local trip working from Bridgwater Yard to serve the Royal Ordnance Factory (ROF) at Puriton. The principal traffic by this date was military explosives and propellants, which was loaded in VEA wagons such as No. 230350. (RLC)

Glimpsed in the reception sidings at Huntspill on 25 September 1989 are No. 47359 and ROF pilot No. 2. The Class 47 is working the local trip up from Bridgwater to exchange traffic with the ROF pilot loco. The ROF pilot No. 2 is one of a pair. Andrew Barclay 0-4-0DH 578 (No. 1), and 0-4-0DH 579 (No. 2) were delivered new to the ROF in 1972. (RLC)

Bridgwater Yard saw an interesting mix of traffic for a small yard. On 12 September 1980 the local trip from Taunton worked by No. 08281 had arrived with a discharged nuclear flask, a sulphuric acid tank for the ROF, and a 16t mineral of scrap to be weighed on the weighbridge in the yard. The vans seen in the yard will be for loading at Puriton ROF, but the empty unfitted 16t minerals are all stored out of use due to the British Steel strike.

By 1981 Bridgwater was served by both a daily Speedlink service from Severn Tunnel Junction and a vacuum-braked service which ran three days a week. On 1 May 1981 No. 31128 arrives at Bridgwater with 7B60, the 08.08 MWFO service from Kingsland Road. The vans will be for loading at the ROF at Puriton, while the KEV wagons have brought rod in coil from AS&W at Cardiff for North Somerset Wire at Bridgwater.

After 1980 the nuclear flask traffic no longer passed to and from Bridgwater on ordinary vacuum-braked services. On 9 August 1983 the dedicated service for nuclear flask traffic 7V52, the 17.22 MWO Sellafield to Bridgwater, is being shunted into the crane compound by No. 47202. The Scammell tractor unit has brought the loaded flask from Hinkley Point.

On 1 May 1981 an additional loco had been requested to work at Bridgwater by the civil engineers. Propelling down through the Up platform is No. 31422 with six grampus wagons of blanketing sand which it is taking to the RSD sidings to the west of the overbridge in the background. The wagons will then be formed up into a train for weekend engineering work.

The daily Speedlink working 6B46, the 06.30 from Severn Tunnel Junction, arrives at Bridgwater on 9 August 1983 behind No. 47327. The train has crossed to the Up platform and is propelling back into the yard. The first five wagons are VGAs in a pool dedicated to load bagged adipic acid from ICI Wilton to Bridgwater. The first production VGA, No. 210401, was one of the five vehicles allocated to the traffic.

In the Speedlink era BR worked with a number of private firms to handle cartage and craneage at various locations. M. Thomas were at Bridgwater (and Plymouth Friary) and as well as unloading fertiliser in the UKF siding they also handled other traffic. Here on 9 September one tonne bags of adipic acid from ICI Wilton are being unloaded from a VGA. Other traffic loaded at this time was cider for Showerings; an Inter-Frigo ferry van of peaches was also unloaded that day.

There were no Speedlink trunk services into the West Country, but important feeder services ran between Severn Tunnel Junction and St Blazey. At Cogload Junction 6C39, the 09.30 St Blazey to Severn Tunnel Junction, passes behind No. 47254 on 25 February 1986. The VEAs behind the loco have probably come from Ernesettle – there are empty PCAs from Barnstaple to Westbury – and the cartic set is returning empty from Exeter St Davids. (RLC)

For many years there was a regular company train from the Blue Circle cement works at Westbury to the Blue Circle depot at Exeter Central. On 13 June 1985 7B22, the 16.05 Westbury to Exeter Central, passes Cogload behind Bath Road-allocated No. 37135, it was unusual to see a Class 37 on this working. The four tracks from here into Taunton were reduced to two in 1986 as part of the Exeter re-signalling scheme. (RLC)

At the start of the decade Class 37s had been rare west of Bristol, as the Bath Road allocation of the class mostly worked stone trains out of Westbury and Tytherington. On 24 August 1981 one of the allocation, No. 37204, arrives at Taunton Fairwater pre-assembly depot with 8X06, a train of recovered track sections from Bristol East depot. In the distance the former Up relief line contains a large number of stored unfitted coal wagons.

At Tiverton Junction No. 50034 *Furious* is working 1A82, the 17.55 FO Plymouth to Paddington service, on 26 July 1985. Heading west is No. 47001 with 8X10, the 18.15 Taunton Fairwater to Exeter Riverside, which is a train of new prefabricated track sections. The remaining stub of the former Hemyock branch curves away on the right. (RLC)

Passing Cowley Bridge Junction on 11 July 1984 is No. 33014 with empty seacow and sealion hoppers forming 6C57 from Exeter Riverside to Meldon Quarry. The metamorphic hornfels rock quarried at Meldon was harder than granite and, depending on demand, up to five or six trains could be loaded each weekday, two of them going forward to the Southern Region.

At Crediton on 31 October 1983 No. 50009 *Conqueror* approaches with 7V80, the 05.35 Salisbury to Meldon Quarry service, which conveys twenty-two empty sealion and seacow ballast hoppers. The semaphore signals here were later replaced as part of the Exeter re-signalling scheme, though the signal box at Crediton remained to control the routes to Barnstaple and Meldon Quarry.

During the annual sugar beet season BR also handled large volumes of beet pulp nuts, which were used as animal feed. In the 1970s special block trains were run from East Anglia to yards across the Western Region. In the Speedlink era little traffic remained and this traditional railway scene would not last much longer. In Barnstaple Yard bags of beet pulp nuts are unloaded from a single VDA No. 210291 on 31 October 1983.

In Exeter freight terminals located at City Basin, Exeter Central, and Exmouth Junction were served by a local trip working based on Exeter Riverside Yard. The diagrammed loco for the working was one of the Laira-allocated Class 08s which were out-based at Exeter. On 9 July 1985 No. 08792 is passing Red Cow Crossing with bitumen tanks from Ellesmere Port for Kings Asphalt at City Basin. Although the tanks are all air-braked a brake van is required for the guard and travelling shunter to ride in.

On 15 July 1986 a short trip from Exeter Riverside Yard runs into Exeter St Davids behind No. 08955. The cartic set conveyed new cars from Fords at Halewood, a regular traffic for many years, while the VGA contains Guinness from Park Royal, which will be unloaded by Premier Transport in the NCL shed. (RLC)

Passing through platform 3 at Exeter St Davids is Class 33/1 No. 33114 with 7V80, the 05.35 Salisbury to Meldon Quarry service on 9 July 1985. The train is formed of empty seacow and sealion ballast hoppers. The Down main line, in the centre, had been taken out of use and lifted as part of the Exeter re-signalling scheme earlier that year.

Standing on the Down main line at Exeter St Davids is No. 50048 *Dauntless* with loaded seacow and sealion ballast hoppers from Meldon Quarry on 11 July 1984. This centre road had always been used by freight trains waiting a banking loco prior to climbing up to Exeter Central, or waiting a pathway to head west. It would be taken out of use the following year, which then made it more difficult to path freight trains through the station.

Since 1981, and the closure of the depot there, the local freight work in the Newton Abbot area was carried out by a daily trip working from Exeter Riverside Yard to Heathfield, and return. On 9 July 1985 No. 33021 is seen approaching Exeter St Davids with the return working. The train comprises two loaded PBA Polybulk clay tigers from ECC Heathfield, and a train of discharged TTAs returning from Heathfield to the Gulf refinery at Waterston.

The carriage and wagon workshops at Exmouth Junction would undertake repair on vehicles of any type that worked into the West Country, as illustrated by this view on 11 March 1983. Cautiously descending the bank from Exeter Central is No. 08941 on local trip duty with a working from Exmouth Junction to Riverside Yard. Meanwhile No. 50041 *Bulwark* works hard up the 1 in 37 gradient with the 14.18 Exeter St Davids to Waterloo service.

The extensive goods yard at Exeter Central had been taken over as a Blue Circle Cement depot. For many years this was served by block company trains of presflos from the Blue Circle plant at Westbury. In the 1980s some cement traffic was also received in PCAs via the Speedlink network, and both types can be seen in this view on 17 July 1985. Premier Transport also moved part of their operation to here, and Guinness was unloaded by the former Fyffes banana warehouse. Two vans can be glimpsed on the right-hand siding.

At Dawlish Warren No. 50007 *Sir Edward Elgar* passes on the Up main with 1A82, the 17.55 FO Plymouth to Paddington service, on 7 June 1985. Standing in the Up loop is the second of the daily Speedlink services from Cornwall, 6C43, the 13.25 service from St Blazey to Severn Tunnel Junction, worked by Crewe Diesel-allocated No. 47214. Polybulk clay tiger PBAs are front and rear, the other two tanks also convey clay traffic, in slurry form. (RLC)

Trainloads of export clay for Switzerland ran fortnightly, two loaded trains each conveying eleven Polybulk hoppers. On 5 November 1981 No. 47094 gets away from Newton Abbot with a loaded train from Tavistock Junction to Dover. The heavy train had been assisted over the South Devon banks by No. 50030 *Repulse*, which had just been detached at Newton Abbot. The returning empties would come back as a combined train of twenty-two wagons.

There were a number of freight terminals in and around Plymouth, served by Class 08-worked trips originating from Tavistock Junction or Plymouth Friary. On 15 November 1982 Laira-allocated No. 08953 heads through Plymouth with a returning trip from the Royal Naval armament depot at Ernesettle to Tavistock Junction. Behind the loco are four VEAs, there were another three towards the rear with a former BR ferry van as a barrier wagon, and a brake van for the guard and travelling shunter.

At Bodmin Road on 15 April 1983 No. 37181 has just run-round a rake of empty clayhoods for Wenford Bridge, and prepares to take them to Boscarne Junction. There they will wait until being worked up to Wenford Bridge the following day by one of the St Blazey-allocated Class 08 locos – the only class of loco permitted to work over that section of line.

Having already detached traffic at Taunton, Exeter Riverside, and Tavistock Junction 6B39, the 05.40 service from Severn Tunnel Junction to Drinnick Mill, is seen approaching Lostwithiel with just three vehicles on 15 November 1982. All three vehicles behind No. 45033 will be for loading with china clay products.

On 23 June 1982 No. 37274 is just departing westwards from the Down loop at Lostwithiel with a train of empty clayhoods from Fowey. In the Unigate depot on the left is a rake of milk tanks, though milk traffic by rail from here had already ceased. These tanks had been refurbished by the Milk Marketing Board in 1981 and were being kept for use in emergency.

Laira-allocated No. 37274 climbs off the Fowey branch into Lostwithiel with a rake of empty clayhoods on 15 November 1982. Between 1954 and 1960 BR built 875 wooden-bodied wagons with end tippler doors for the export traffic via Fowey. Constant problems with water ingress under the flat tarpaulins led to the modification of some wagons from 1974 with a tarpaulin bar, which gave the wagons their distinctive hood shape.

At Par on 21 April 1982 No. 37142 has just run-round a short train comprising one MCV (16t min) and one MDV (21t min), which are loaded with domestic coal for St Austell goods yard. Domestic coal, along with scrap and cement, were among the last traffic types handled on the vacuum-braked wagon load network, which would finally close in April 1984.

In 1983 Laira depot had five Class 37s allocated, principally to work china clay traffic in Cornwall. One of them, No. 37181, is stabled in the yard at St Blazey on 7 November 1983 with a variety of clay wagons. There are three Polybulk hoppers, a PAA covhop (one of nine operated by Tullis Russel to convey clay from Goonbarrow to Markinch), and a pair of PBA clay tigers.

Class 25s had been allocated to Laira depot since 1971 when the first arrivals displaced the last Class 22 diesel hydraulics. Thereafter there were typically ten to twelve members of the class allocated, and they worked many of the clay trips in Cornwall until 1980. On 16 July 1980 No. 25155 is seen stabled at St Blazey with a train of clayhoods. On the left No. 37142 was one of the first replacement Class 37s in the area. By November that year the last Class 25 had left, and No. 25155 was withdrawn from traffic on 1 December 1980.

The first Class 46 locos to be allocated to the Western Region went to Bath Road in 1971, with Laira receiving six members in 1972. Although there were twenty-five allocated to Laira in 1980, they were rapidly withdrawn or allocated away. Members of the class had often worked freight traffic in Cornwall and on 16 July 1980 one of the Laira allocation No. 46020 is stabled at St Blazey depot.

A number of the china clay loading points lay west of St Austell along the branch from Burngullow to Parkandillack. On 15 April 1983 No. 37274 heads west towards St Austell with empty clayhoods from Fowey. The connection from St Austell goods yard can be seen on the left, and in the distance are chimneys at Par Harbour.

By 1983 regular freight traffic in West Cornwall was becoming rare, it included domestic coal to Ponsandane, cement to Chacewater and traction fuel to Long Rock depot. On 8 March 1983 No. 50025 *Invincible* heads east through Truro with a Penzance to St Blazey Speedlink trip, conveying empty PCAs from Chacewater to Blue Circle Plymstock and discharged TTAs from Long Rock for Fawley refinery.

On 25 September 1986 6C39, the 09.30 from St Blazey, passes through Severn Tunnel Junction station behind No. 47378. The train comprises discharged bitumen TTAs, Polybulks of clay, empty PCAs and an empty cartic set from Exeter St Davids to Halewood. Severn Tunnel Junction was an important location on the Speedlink Network, with services on routes to Dover, Doncaster, Tees/Tyne, Mossend and Harwich.

A view of the Down hump yard at Severn Tunnel Junction on 16 June 1983, as seen looking west from the road overbridge that spanned the yard. A mix of air-braked and vacuum-braked stock is visible including engineers traffic. On the left, the concrete pad was used for wagon repairs, while to the right the small loco depot can be seen on the Up side, across the main lines.

With freight services arriving at Severn Tunnel Junction from across all regions of BR, unsurprisingly a wide variety of locos could be seen there, as in this view of the loco depot on 20 July 1985. Locos present include Nos 08668 (Canton), 31154 and 45004 (both Toton), and 47235 another Canton-allocated loco. (RLC)

Allied Steel & Wire at Cardiff were an important Railfreight customer, as well as dispatching steel products inbound scrap was received. On 25 September 1986 former Stratford-allocated No. 47112 (by now a Canton-allocated loco) passes Undy Yard at Severn Tunnel Junction with a train of scrap in MDVs for Cardiff Tidal Sidings. By this date MDVs were commonly used for scrap traffic, having previously been used almost exclusively for coal traffic.

At Undy, running on the Up relief line is No. 37180 *Sir Dyfed/County of Dyfed* with a mixed vacuum-braked service for Severn Tunnel Junction on 16 June 1983. The front portion of the train is formed by three MCVs and a long rake of HTVs loaded with house coal, the rear of the train comprises a mix of wagon types.

No Class 25s had been allocated to the WR since 1980 but they were still regular visitors to the region. At Llanwern Works West Connection, on 10 February 1982, Longsight-allocated No. 25211 heads east along the Up main line with a train of empty BDAs. The loco was later transferred to Bescot, and then Crewe Diesel, and was not withdrawn from traffic until June 1986. It was one of the last of the class to be scrapped, not being broken up until 1995.

A named pair of Canton-allocated Class 56s, Nos 56037 *Richard Trevithick* and 56038 *Western Mail,* approach Llanwern Works West Connection with an empty iron ore set from Llanwern for Port Talbot on 10 February 1982. Pairs of Class 56s had first been diagrammed to these workings in August 1979 when they replaced triple-headed Class 37s, the train length being increased from twenty-seven to thirty wagons. Two sets of wagons generally worked three round trips each weekday.

The 9C07 Moreton on Lugg to Severn Tunnel Junction service stands in the Down relief at Hereford station on 12 February behind No. 47285. The train had earlier arrived from Moreton on Lugg with just the single van behind the loco. Most of the vehicles attached at Hereford were empty BDAs that had delivered steel section for Painter Brothers private siding.

Standing on the Down relief line at Hereford on 7 February 1986 is newly converted ex-works Class 37/4 No. 37427. It is working 6V75, the 06.05 Mossend to Severn Tunnel Junction service, conveying coil from Ravenscraig loaded on BAAs and BBAs. The loco had just been released from Crewe Works after being converted from No. 37288 and would receive the name *Bont y Bermo* in April 1986. (RLC)

The three refineries at Milford Haven despatched traffic to oil terminals across a wide area. Murco Petroleum operated terminals at Bedworth, Theale and Westerleigh all served from Robeston. On 23 February 1983 Bath Road-allocated No. 47138 crosses the River Usk at Newport with 6Z32, the 04.45 Robeston to Bedworth service.

By 1985 unfitted traffic had ceased to run in many parts of the BR network, but in South Wales several traffic flows continued to use unfitted wagons. Export coil from Llanwern to Newport Docks crosses the River Usk behind No. 37204 on 7 May 1985. The first six vehicles are unfitted coil J wagons, modified former iron ore tipplers now coded KJO on the TOPS system. The train also conveyed coil C wagons (TOPS code KCO).

Cardiff Canton had an allocation of nine Class 56 locos for use on iron ore traffic from Port Talbot to Llanwern, as well as some petroleum traffic from West Wales. Toton-allocated No. 56064 was therefore an unusual visitor in South Wales when seen in multiple with Canton-allocated No. 56032 *Sir De Morgannwg/ County of South Glamorgan*. The train is 6Z43, the 17.30 Llanwern to Port Talbot, seen passing Newport on 2 July 1985. (RLC)

During weekday afternoons Severn Tunnel Junction received a number of important Speedlink trips and feeder services, which connected into evening departures heading across the network. One service, which was regularly heavily loaded, was 6C42, the 15.50 Cardiff Tidal Sidings to Severn Tunnel Junction. On 12 July 1985 6C42 passes through Newport behind No. 37230, as usual steel products from Allied Steel & Wire form the bulk of the load.

Passing Newport on 30 June 1988 on the Up main line is No. 37176 with 6B76, the 19.10 Ebbw Vale to Llanwern service. The train conveys a selection of new PXA wagons recently built by Powell Duffryn. At this date there were six timetabled services on weekdays from Waunllwyd North (the yard that served BSC Ebbw Vale tinplate works), they could run on a 'Y' pathway to either Llanwern or Severn Tunnel Junction. (RLC)

Following the creation of the Railfreight Metals in 1987 the sub-sector operated a number of long-distance services. Thornaby depot had an allocation of over twenty Class 37/5s for metals traffic and two of them are seen at Newport. On 4 July 1989 Nos 37520 and 37509 head east with 6E47, the 11.00 Cardiff Tidal Sidings to Tees Yard service. (RLC)

The BSC Ebbw Vale works ceased making steel in the 1970s and the site was developed as a tinplate works processing hot rolled coil imported from other BSC plants. On 4 September 1984 No. 37176 passes through Newport heading for Ebbw Vale with three loaded BAAs of coil, and an empty VCA.

The Shellstar palvans operated by UKF Fertilisers were a familiar site on the WR, passing on trains to depots in the West Country as well as Carmarthen. On 2 July 1985 No. 47307 passes Newport with 6Z35, the 11.30 Ince & Elton to Carmarthen. The front portion of the train is formed of PWA palvans, but the rear comprises OCAs loaded with one tonne bags of fertiliser, a method of conveyance which had become common in recent years. (RLC)

Class 50s were less commonly employed on freight traffic, and a Class 50 freight working in South Wales was quite unusual. On 19 July 1989 No. 50015 *Valiant* worked 6Z04 from Bridgwater British Cellophane through to Cardiff Tidal Sidings with discharged tanks. The train is seen at Newport where a conductor driver was provided for the journey into Cardiff Tidal, No. 37897 is on the adjacent line. (RLC)

In the Western Valleys Marine and Oakdale were the last two collieries to remain rail connected. East Usk was the yard responsible for supplying coal empties for the area, though in later years empties ran direct from Llanwern. On 2 July 1985 6A76, the 15.55 East Usk to Marine service, formed of empty MDVs, passes through Newport behind No. 37248. (RLC)

Coking coal for Llanwern had traditionally been loaded in MDVs, but by the mid-1980s they were joined by HTVs displaced from domestic coal traffic by the newer HBAs and HEAs. On 25 September 1986 Canton-allocated No. 37508 approaches Newport with 7A73 Marine to Llanwern with coal in HTVs. The 37/5 had been converted from split-headcode 37/0 No. 37090, which would have been a rare visitor to South Wales in its previous guise.

BR built 225 Cov-ABs with centre only doors, these were coded VCA on TOPS and were principally used on tinplate traffic from Trostre, Velindre and Ebbw Vale. On 7 May 1985 No. 37224 exits Newport New Tunnel with a Severn Tunnel Junction to Ebbw Vale service, the first three vehicles are empty VCAs.

To handle coil traffic BR converted many unfitted wagons, with former 20t pig iron wagons becoming coil C (TOPS code KCO), and former 24t tippler wagons becoming coil J (TOPS code KJO). Baulks of timber were fitted to help secure the coils. On 7 May 1985 No. 37204 heads past Gaer Junction towards Newport Old Tunnel with empty KCOs and KJOs from Newport Docks on the short journey to Llanwern.

Scrap traffic to Allied Steel & Wire at Cardiff had brought March-allocated No. 37216 to South Wales. It is seen here on 7 May 1985 passing Gaer Junction with returning empty MCVs from Cardiff Tidal Sidings to Whitemoor Yard.

Coil for Ebbw Vale loaded on BAAs and BBAs leaves Gaer Junction and approaches Gaer Tunnel behind No. 37254 on 19 May 1982. The section of line to Park Junction had been singled, and recovered track sections are piled outside the tunnel on the formation of the former Down line.

A busy scene at Gaer Junction on 1 December 1981 as No. 37184 descends the bank from Park Junction with MDVs of coal for Llanwern. Meanwhile No. 37176 is held on the Down relief line awaiting acceptance into A. D. Junction (Alexandra Dock Junction Yard) with export coil for Newport Docks loaded in unfitted KCOs and KJOs.

Approaching Park Junction is Canton-allocated No. 37508 with empty HTVs from Llanwern to Marine on 25 September 1986. Coal from nearby Six Bells Colliery was also loaded at Marine, there were four planned train paths each weekday to Llanwern or Margam. Unfortunately, geological faults in the coal seams hampered production and Marine Colliery closed in March 1989, the last deep mine to work in the Ebbw Valleys.

Track ballast for the WR had been loaded at Tintern/Tidenham and Hirwaun, but by 1986 only Machen Quarry was still supplying ballast in South Wales. On 25 September 1986 the Park Junction signal man collects the token from the crew of No. 37181. The train consists of eleven loaded dogfish ballast hoppers with a pair of loaded sealions on the rear. There were normally two booked trains from Machen on weekdays at this date, both running from and to Severn Tunnel Junction.

On 12 July 1985 a train of steel slab from Port Talbot heads east past A.D. Junction Yard behind No. 45026, the majority of the wagons in the train are BBAs. The yard contains mostly vacuum-braked traffic, including a train of coal in MDVs as well as assorted rakes of MDVs and HTVs. The portacabin on the left was, at one time, the home of Newport TOPS office.

Cardiff Canton-allocated No. 37150 passes the site of Ebbw Junction depot with 7B66, the 11.12 from Oakdale with loaded HAAs, on 12 July 1985. Ebbw Junction depot had closed in 1982 with locos subsequently stabled at Godfrey Road adjacent to Newport station. In 1986 No. 37150 entered Crewe Works and was converted to Class 37/9 No. 37901.

A view of A.D. Junction yard looking east as No. 37177 passes on the Down relief with a lengthy train of presflos from Severn Tunnel Junction on 12 July 1985. Aberthaw Cement had been an important freight customer with cement works at Aberthaw and Roose despatching cement to terminals in Carmarthen, Bristol, Taunton, and Exeter.

On the afternoon of 17 September 1981 Gateshead-allocated No. 47405 is seen in the reception sidings at Pengam Freightliner terminal, having earlier arrived with 4E70, the Danygraig to Stratford service. Meanwhile Tinsley-allocated No. 45015 is in the terminal shunting to form up the other evening departures, which will be the 4S81 to Coatbridge, and 4E88 to Newcastle.

Cardiff Canton-allocated No. 37278 passes through Cardiff Central on the Down main line with 6B74, the 17. 45 East Usk to Llantrisant service, comprising empty HTVs on 19 May 1986. Llantrisant was the focal point for local trips serving collieries and coking plants at Cwm and Coed Ely, as well as the opencast site at Llanharan. The linked collieries of Cwm/Coed Ely would close in November 1986. (RLC)

Didcot Power Station received coal from South Wales from time to time. Initially trains were powered by a Class 47, though later the use of Class 56 locos enabled to load to be increased to forty-five HAAs. It was necessary for trains to be assisted through the Severn Tunnel, with the assisting engine detaching at Stoke Gifford. On 19 May 1986 Nos 37177 and 56065 head through Cardiff Central with 6A10, the 19.25 Margam to Didcot Power Station, with coal from Parc Slip. (RLC)

In the Speedlink era the Isis Link distribution depot at Canton was served by a local trip working from Cardiff Tidal Sidings, worked by a Canton-allocated Class 08. On 24 June 1982 No. 08193 is heading east through Cardiff Central with the return trip to Tidal Sidings. Traffic handled there included steel coil, aluminium slab, and train ferry traffic from the continent.

There were two Freightliner terminals in South Wales, at Pengam to the east of Cardiff, and Danygraig to the east of Swansea Docks. In earlier years there had been several booked departures each weekday from Danygraig, but by 1985 4E70, the 16.15 service to Stratford, was the only regular departure. On 7 May 1985 4E70 passes through Cardiff Central on the Up main line behind No. 47234 as Class 117 Pressed Steel DMU set No. L418 waits in platform 2.

A large tonnage of steel was moved between British Steel plants within South Wales and beyond. On 19 May 1986 6A85, the 12.40 Llanwern to Margam service, is seen passing westwards through Cardiff Central, it is formed of BAAs and BBAs loaded with coil. Loco No. 45029 was allocated to Toton depot, as were all twenty-three remaining members of Class 45/0 by this date. (RLC)

Although pairs of Canton-allocated Class 56s had been diagrammed to the Port Talbot to Llanwern iron ore services since 1979 Class 37s were still sometimes seen on the workings for various reasons. On 19 May 1986 Nos 37208 and 37189 head east through Cardiff Central with empties on 6C41, the 12.05 service from Llanwern to Port Talbot. Interestingly this pair of locos were allocated to Bath Road at the time. (RLC)

Until 1981 the goods depot at Canton was operated by Cory and served by a local trip from Newtown Yard located to the east of Cardiff Central. Here on 22 May 1980 a returning trip from the Cory freight depot passes Cardiff Central behind one of Cardiff Canton's large allocation of Class 08s, No. 08350. By this date vacuum-braked general merchandise traffic was in decline, and Newtown Yard would close in 1981.

Shunting at Deep Navigation colliery on 24 May 1983 is the NCB pilot loco. It is EEV D919, an 0-6-0DH shunting loco dating from 1965 which had formerly worked at Penallta colliery. It is shunting a rake of HKVs, 34t former iron ore hoppers, which are loaded with colliery shale which will be taken to the Nelson Bog tip at Penallta Junction for disposal.

One of Cardiff Canton's remaining vacuum only Class 37s No. 37251 is seen at Deep Navigation colliery on 24 May 1983 with a train of HKVs of colliery shale for Nelson Bog at Penallta Junction. The HKVs had originally been built to convey iron ore from Newport Docks to Llanwern steelworks.

At Radyr Yard on 16 February 1983 is a sight once quite common in yards across the BR network. MDV No. B312055 and a similar wagon have been subject to a heavy shunt resulting in a buffer stop collision and derailment. This wagon was one of a large number built to diagram No. 1/120 from 1962 to 1964 and was one of a large batch originally allocated to work in South Wales.

Radyr Yard was the principal yard for wagon load traffic in the Cardiff Valleys. A number of Canton Class 08s were out-based at Radyr to shunt the yard and work local trips, including to Cathays Carriage and wagon shops. On 26 June 1981 No. 08195 arrives back at Radyr with a lengthy rake of wagons from Cathays, while the coal wagons on the right are a shunt move being made by the Radyr yard pilot.

On 24 May 1983 one of the Class 37s out-based at Radyr for local freight work No. 37162 approaches Taffs Well with a train of coal from Tower colliery for export via Swansea Docks. The Taff Vale Railway main line had been four tracked as far as Pontypridd, but declining mineral traffic meant that the route between Taffs Well and Pontypridd had been reduced to double track in 1980.

Some of the coal movement in South Wales was between collieries, washeries and processing plants. At Pontypridd No. 37218 has just run-round a train of mixed coal empties from the Phurnacite plant at Abercwmboi and is departing north for one of the collieries in the Rhondda Valley on 3 November 1981.

The route from Abercynon to Merthyr Tydfil had been singled in 1971 with a passing loop at Black Lion. On 14 April 1983 No. 37231 is shunting at Black Lion Loop to form up a train of coal from Merthyr Vale colliery. It will then depart for the Phurnacite plant at Abercwmboi, travelling via Pontypridd to reverse.

Coal from Merthyr Vale colliery had to be hauled up a steep connecting line to Black Lion Loop on the Merthyr Tydfil line. The NCB employed two former BR Class 08 shunting locos at Merthyr Vale, Nos D3014 and D3183. On 14 April 1983 No. D3014 hauls HTVs of coal up the connecting line to Black Lion Loop. Merthyr Vale colliery closed in 1989, and only six deep mines remained in production at the end of the decade.

Coal for Aberthaw Power Station originated at a number of collieries and blending sites, each train formed of twenty-eight HAAs. The services were worked by pairs of Class 37s with six pairs of locos out-based at Barry. On 21 July 1982 Nos 37224 and 37186 power through Barry with a loaded train for Aberthaw. The introduction of the refurbished heavyweight Class 37/7s meant that trains could then be worked by a single loco.

Aberthaw Cement forwarded cement from plants at Aberthaw and Rhoose. On 7 May 1985 a train of cement in PCAs had earlier been brought into Barry by No. 47359, and after loco change the train is seen departing Barry behind Nos 37235 and 37223.

Approaching Barry from the Vale of Glamorgan route is a ballast train hauled by No. 37243 on 17 September 1981. The seven hoppers are newly built seacow ballast hoppers in the recently introduced yellow and grey 'Dutch' livery. Seacow hoppers were an air-braked only version of the sealion and were built at Shildon and Ashford between 1981 and 1982.

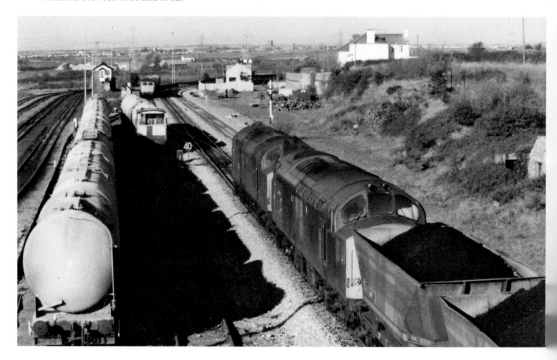

Arriving at Aberthaw Reception sidings on 12 November 1985 are No. 37254 and 37181 with 7Z66, the 09.15 special working from Oakdale. The Class 37s will be detached here, and the slow speed fitted Class 47 seen in the distance will work the train into Aberthaw Power Station to unload.

An afternoon Speedlink service from Fishguard Harbour to Severn Tunnel Junction is seen at Water Street Junction east of Margam on 12 November 1985 behind No. 37256. The former BR ferry van behind the loco is acting as a barrier wagon to the VEAs which are loaded with munitions from the Royal Naval armaments depot at Trecwn.

Some of the coal loading points for Aberthaw Power Station were to the west, at Blaenant, and Steel Supply at Jersey Marine. On 12 November 1985 Nos 37177 and 37126 head 7C83, the 11.40 service from Jersey Marine to Aberthaw, past Water Street Junction. (RLC)

The oil refinery at Llandarcy opened in 1922 and was the first large refinery in Britain. Inverness-allocated No. 37146 was an unusual visitor to South Wales in 1986. It is seen passing Port Talbot on 19 September 1986 with 6C13, the Llandarcy to Severn Tunnel Junction Speedlink service.

On 19 September 1986 Swansea Burrows pilot No. 08780 shunts a train of export coal in MDOs which had recently arrived from Onllwyn. These wagons were among 2500 vehicles that had been re-bodied in 1975 and 1976 specifically for use in South Wales. The use of unfitted wagons on export coal through Swansea Docks was one of the last unfitted traffic flows on BR, lasting until early 1987.

As well as export coal Swansea Burrows sidings handled traffic for a number of other customers, including the Fords factory, Gower Chemicals, and the Port Tennant Wagon Repairs workshop. On 19 September 1986 Swansea Burrows pilot No. 08780 is at work in the 'A' set sidings shunting Fords traffic. The cranes of Danygraig Freightliner terminal are visible in the distance.

Swansea Docks pilot No. 08259 moves MDOs of export coal from the holding sidings past Kings Dock Junction signal box towards the hoists on 9 November 1983. Unfitted wagons were used for this traffic, they were each uncoupled and lifted individually on the coal hoist. At one time there were over thirty coal hoists in the docks, but only four remained in operation by the 1980s.

On 19 September 1986 Swansea Docks pilot No. 08367 hauls loaded MDOs of export coal from Swansea Burrows towards the Violet Sidings where they will be held until called for unloading. The final coal hoist in use was last used in February 1987, after which date coal traffic was grab discharged from MDVs or exported in containers.

The Burry Port & Gwendraeth Valley line to Coed Bach and Cwmmawr had a number of low bridges, the only locos capable of working the route were modified Class 03s which had cut-down cabs. On 15 June 1983 three of Landore depot's modified Class 03s, Nos 03141, 03145, and 03152, are seen at Pembrey and Burry Port having just arrived with a loaded train. The Class 08 No. 08354 was the Pembrey and Burry Port yard pilot.

From the 1960s the oil refineries at Milford Haven had provided important petroleum traffic for BR. One terminal that was served for many years by the Gulf refinery at Waterston was the Albion terminal in the West Midlands. On 6 June 1983 Bath Road-allocated No. 47245 accelerates through Whitland with 6M50, the 15.30 service from Waterston to Albion.

Anthracite produced by collieries at Abernant, Betws drift mine and Gwaun-cae-Gurwen provided work for a number of Class 08 and Class 37s locos out-based at Pantyffynnon. Coal was moved to Wernos washery, and also large tonnages went to Swansea Docks for export as well as to coal depots across BR. On 4 November 1983 Landore-allocated No. 08799 is seen shunting in the yard at Pantyffynnon.

Freight operations in the Pantyffynnon area were based at the station, where there was a traincrew signing on point, while a loco stabling point was located adjacent to the station. On 24 June 1982 No. 37304 is shut down at the stabling point while No. 37267 has just arrived from Llandeilo Junction with a short train of domestic coal. The yard pilot No. 08660 is stabled to the rear of Pantyffynnon station.

Although Wernos Drift Mine had closed in 1965 Wernos Washery continued to process coal from other sources in the area until closure in 1988. The reception sidings for Wernos Washery lay immediately north of Pantyffynnon station, to the west of the Central Wales line. On 24 June 1982 the signal is cleared for No. 08660 to proceed from Pantyffynnon to collect traffic from Wernos. A rake of MDOs can be seen in the distance.